Animal Fairy Tales

Ratpunzel

written by Charlotte Guillain ☆ illustrated by Dawn Beacon

Raintree

Chicago, Illinois

Edited by Daniel Nunn, Rebecca Rissman, and Catherine Veitch
Designed by Joanna Hinton-Malivoire
Original illustrations © Capstone Global Library, Ltd, 2014
Illustrated by Dawn Beacon
Production by Victoria Fitzgerald
Originated by Capstone Global Library, Ltd
Printed and bound in China

17 16 15 14 13
10 9 8 7 6 5 4 3 2 1

Library of Congress Cataloging-in-Publication Data
Guillain, Charlotte.
  Ratpunzel / Charlotte Guillain.
      pages cm.—(Animal fairy tales)
  ISBN 978-1-4109-6112-9 (hb)—ISBN 978-1-4109-6119-8 (pb) [1. Fairy tales. 2. Folklore—
Germany.] I. Rapunzel. English. II. Title.
  PZ8.G947Rat 2014
  398.2—dc22   2013011756
  [E]

Characters

Ratpunzel

Mother and Father

Cruel Cat

Prince Ratdolph

Once upon a time, there were two rats
who loved each other very much.
One day the wife became sick.

"Please fetch some special seeds from
the forest for me to eat," she begged
her husband. He did as she asked for
two nights, and she began to get better.

On the third night, the husband went
back to the forest to fetch more seeds,
but he was caught by a cruel cat.
He begged for mercy.

"I will let you go if you promise to
give me your first baby," purred the
cat. Terrified, the husband agreed and
scurried away.

Time passed and the couple had
a baby daughter.
They named her Ratpunzel.

One morning the cat appeared.
"You must keep your promise and
give me the child," said the cat,
taking Ratpunzel away.

Ratpunzel grew up into a beautiful rat, with a very long tail. The cat hid Ratpunzel away in a tall tower, deep in the forest.

Only the cat could visit her, by climbing up Ratpunzel's tail.

Ratpunzel had a beautiful voice, and
she would spend her time singing
at the top of the tower. One day,
handsome Prince Ratdolph was riding
through the forest.

Prince Ratdolph heard Ratpunzel
singing. He followed the sound and saw
the cat climbing up Ratpunzel's tail.

Prince Ratdolph came back that night.
"Let down your tail!" he called like
the cat. Ratpunzel did as he asked, and
Prince Ratdolph climbed up into the tower.

Prince Ratdolph and Ratpunzel fell in
love. He visited her every night, taking
thread for Ratpunzel to weave into a
ladder to escape.

Time passed and Ratpunzel had almost finished weaving the ladder for her escape.

One morning the cat came to visit her. "You're so much heavier to pull up than the prince," puffed Ratpunzel.

The cat was furious that Prince Ratdolph had visited. He sent Ratpunzel out into the forest.

That night, Prince Ratdolph came to see Ratpunzel as usual. The cat pulled him up by using a rope.

"You will never see Ratpunzel again!" he snarled when the prince reached the top of the tower. The prince jumped from the tower to escape.

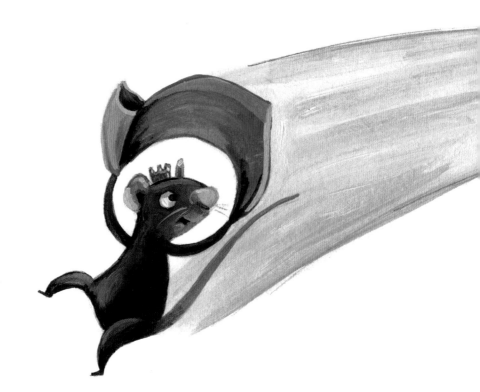

Prince Ratdolph landed in a thornbush, which scratched his eyes and blinded him. He wandered in the deep, dark forest day and night, unable to see.

But one day he heard
a familiar voice
singing beautifully.

Prince Ratdolph followed the voice into a clearing, where he fell into Ratpunzel's paws. She wept when she saw his scratched eyes. Magically, her tears brought his sight back.

Prince Ratdolph and Ratpunzel were married and lived happily ever after.

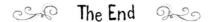 The End

Where does this story come from?

You've probably already heard the story that *Ratpunzel* is based on—*Rapunzel*. There are many different versions of this story. When people tell a story, they often make little changes to make it their own. How would you change this story?

The history of the story

Rapunzel was first written down by the Brothers Grimm. Jacob (1785–1863) and Wilhelm (1786–1859) Grimm lived near the city of Frankfurt, in Germany. They collected and wrote down many fairy stories and folktales. These tales were told by storytellers who entertained people in the days before radio and television.

In the original story, a husband and wife live next to a witch. The wife is pregnant and craves a plant called rapunzel from the witch's garden, so her husband goes to fetch it for her. But on the third night, the witch catches him and makes him promise her his unborn child. The promise is kept, and the witch names the baby Rapunzel. The girl grows up to be beautiful with long golden hair, so the witch hides her away in a tall tower with no door or stairs. Only the witch can enter the tower by climbing Rapunzel's hair. A prince hears Rapunzel singing and learns how to climb up to see her. They fall in love and plan Rapunzel's escape, but she accidentally gives the plan away to the witch. The witch cuts off Rapunzel's hair and casts her out into the forest. When the prince visits, the witch lets down Rapunzel's cut hair and pulls him up into the tower. When he discovers what has happened, he jumps from the tower and is blinded by a thornbush. As he wanders through the forest, he eventually hears Rapunzel singing and they are reunited. Her loving tears restore his sight, and they live happily ever after.